---------*-------

Intentionally left blank

---------*-------

Supported by:

Laihui Play Pena (Pp) Class, Manipur.

Thawai Hou Arts and Event Space, Heibongpokpi, Manipur

Published by:

Marjing Mayanglambam
Founder We Can Change Manipur (WCCM)

Contributors can contact us through email for any details :

wecanchangemanipur@gmail.com

Editorial notes

Errors are bound to happen since we are all humans. Please correct us in a very positive way so that we can accept your correction in a more mature and cultured manner. This is just the beginning, and WCCM is open to doing more work with groups and communities who are less extreme and do not use propaganda suited for their external affiliations.

Achangba Khunai Amagi damak, WCCM is ready for any work.

Thagatchari (Thank you)

Editorial Board Members,

We Can Change Manipur (WCCM), Imphal

12/12/2023 - Tuesday

Happy Readings and seeing!

---------*-------

Intentionally Left Blank

---------*-------

LET ME STAY IN PAIN

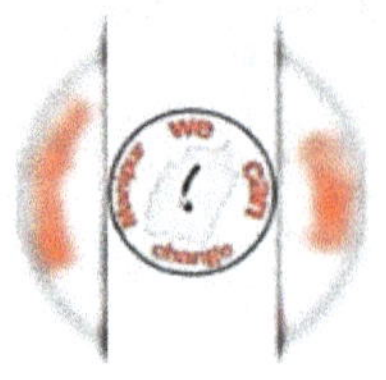

BY MEGHABARNA THIYAM

WE CAN CHANGE MANIPUR-WCCM

wccm2024 "Let me stay in pain"

Let me stay in pain
As it keeps me sane,
From the illusions of this world
That makes my head twirl.
When in pain , my mind is clear
Helps me think and kicks out fear.
It keeps my energy on focus
Towards the things that matter.
These storms of fogs and locust,
Tries to distract me with their chatter
But the pain helps me see through
And steers my mind on what's true.

– Meghabarna Thiyam

---------*-------

Intentionally Left Blank

---------*-------

ASIBA THAWAIGI ACHANGBA MAMI

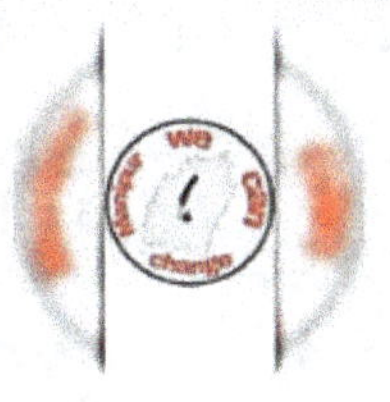

BY ANDREW LAIPHRAKPAM

WE CAN CHANGE MANIPUR-WCCM

Chatkhare mahakti ningamdana
Akanba ereina humduna pubikhre
Kallaba malem gi tamthiraba nongleina
Humduna pubikhare nungsiraba thawai mahak
Mapham keida chattuna thiba dasu phanglaroi,
Asibi thawaigi achangba Mami
Amuk tadi hallakkhogaba, he nungsiraba thawai
Ngasigi taibangpal asida mutnaidana leihouragani
Ngna thambiramba nungsi khudol kaya ase
Kaoba ngamlaroidaba nggi mamal yamlaba wahei
kaya,
Asibi thawaigi achangba Mami
Ningsingbada ngaihouragani kaongamdraba
thoudok
kaya kaya,
Awaba, nungaiba kaya kayana oihankhi punsi
amagi
masak
Ahal oiraklaba matam hedo nahe challaba matam
faoba
Thambirammi ningsing khudam oinabani haiduna
Asiba Thawaigi achangba Mami
Chatloko nahakti swarga gi leikolda
Khongjom nubi taret ka sanajaruro
Sanajaruro nungaiba ipak amada
Chaktajaruro napang laktaa
Asiba Thawaigi achangba Mami
Chatloko He Thawai

---------*-------

Intentionally Left Blank

---------*-------

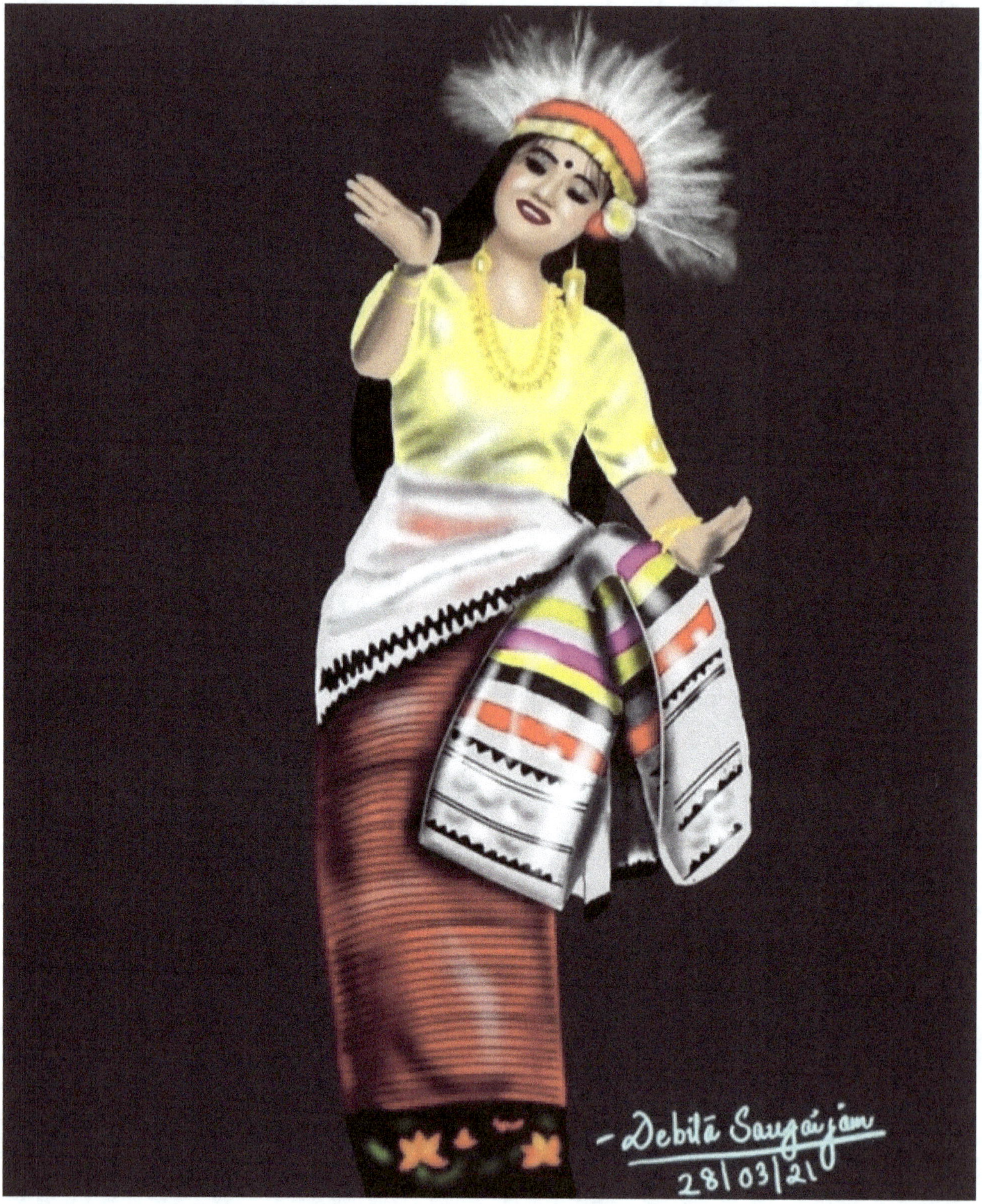
-Debitā Saugaijam
28/03/21

---------*-------

Intentionally Left Blank

---------*-------

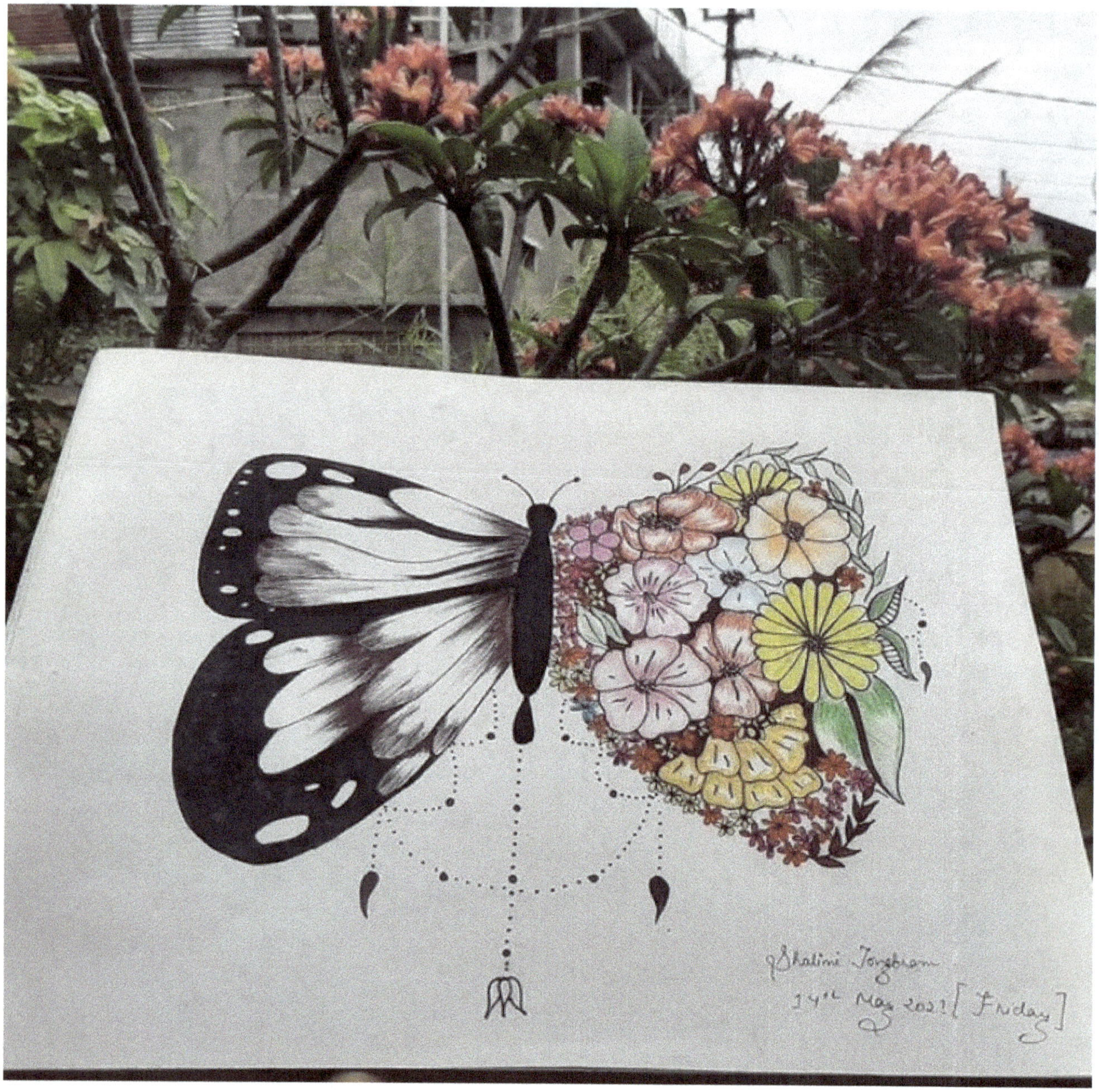
Shalini Jongbam
14th May 2021 [Friday]

---------*-------

Intentionally Left Blank

---------*-------

Naorem Keishomba

General Secretary (WCCM)

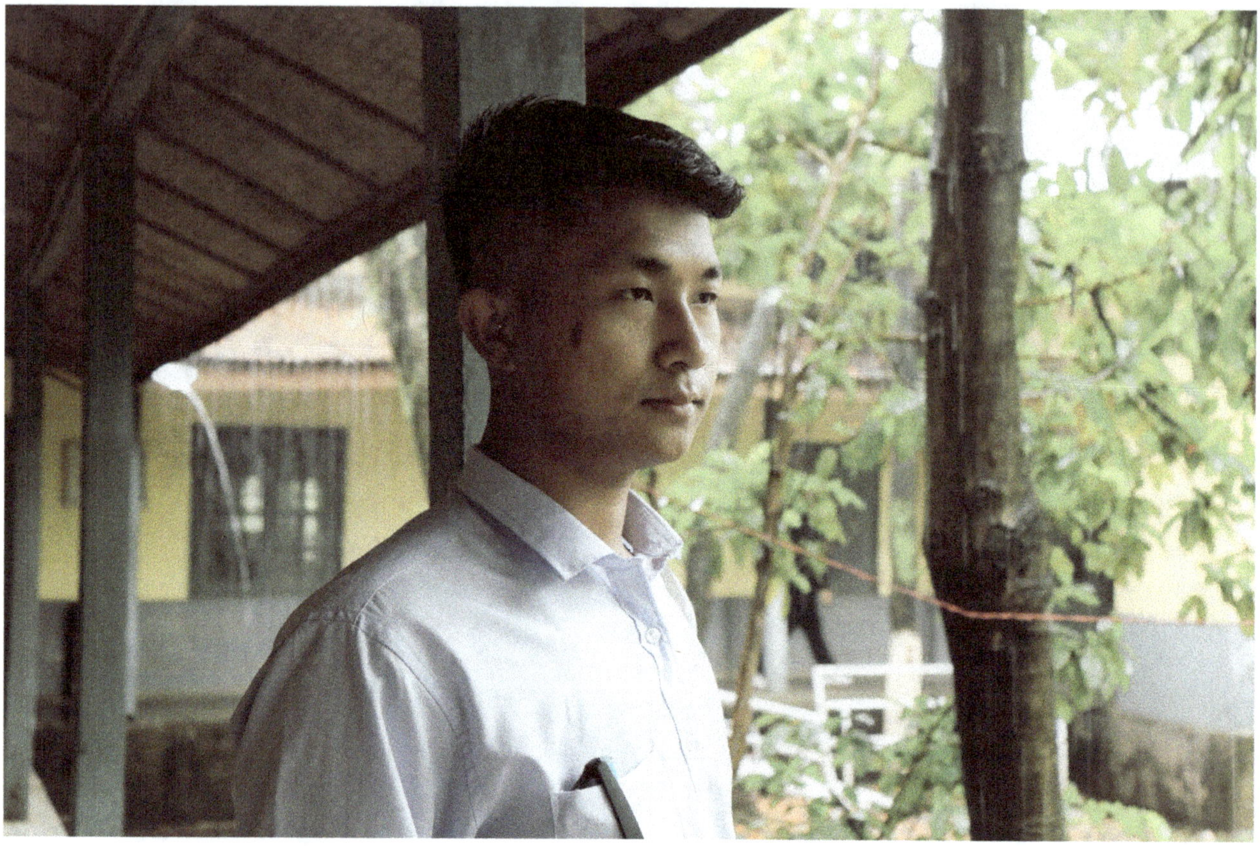

REVIVAL

Lonliness is not our nature,
Since God has made us for one another
So only my opinion is not that just;
For unified satisfaction is also must.
Even if I tried to stand alone
But the thought of collective good always drag my backbone,
Besides all these factors, the world badly needs a revival;
Can't do it myself at my own risk
Without all this conceptional.
Our ambience which one filled with peace and harmony;
Dismayed by the collectives terror of science and technology.
Replacing old ones by the contemporary and leaving behind astounding nature's beauty.
Time passed by continuing it own cycle;
Wondering why it associate with such grieved results.
All these changes compelled me to flow along with them
With me as part of it, flowing endlessly down the stream.
Leaving the present abandoned to presume for future;
As if we all have been assigned to destroy the nature.
Now things have been recast in such a traumatic way;
That no man had ever dreamed of,
Even in their gloomiest day.
Word are limitless for describing ;
The devastation cause by this modern civilisation.

- Naorem Keishomba

Jonyson Salamcha

Public Relations & Management Secretary (WCCM)

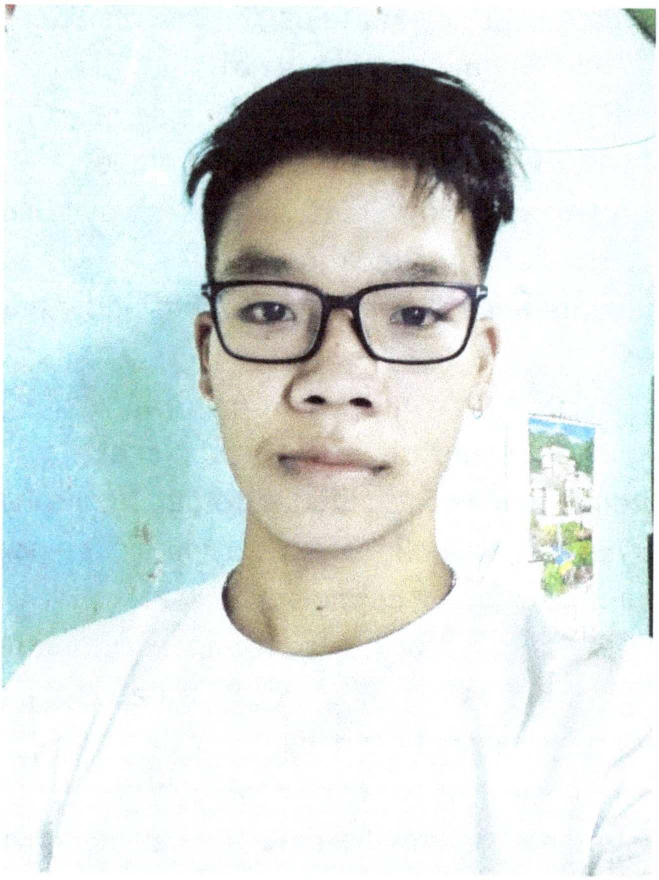

A TRUE WAY OF LIFE

Let's think about the thought
Of sympathy, and
Of the same accord.
Then, emulate like the work
Of a brave person,
And an honest person.

Always concentrate in what
You're doing; otherwise,
It may lead to fruitless life.
Always do your bounden duty
Sincerely; then, you'll be loved
By all human in the end.

Let's make a lot of singing tune
That makes heart pleasant,
Blows minds in a happy moment.
Also, let's sing a song along
With a dance that's congenial
To the song with lyrics to be beautiful.

Finally, let's perform good deeds
In life. And turn it into an endless
Glory : that can make the new ones
Able to give a true way of life.

- Jonyson Salamcha

---------*-------

Intentionally Left Blank

---------*-------

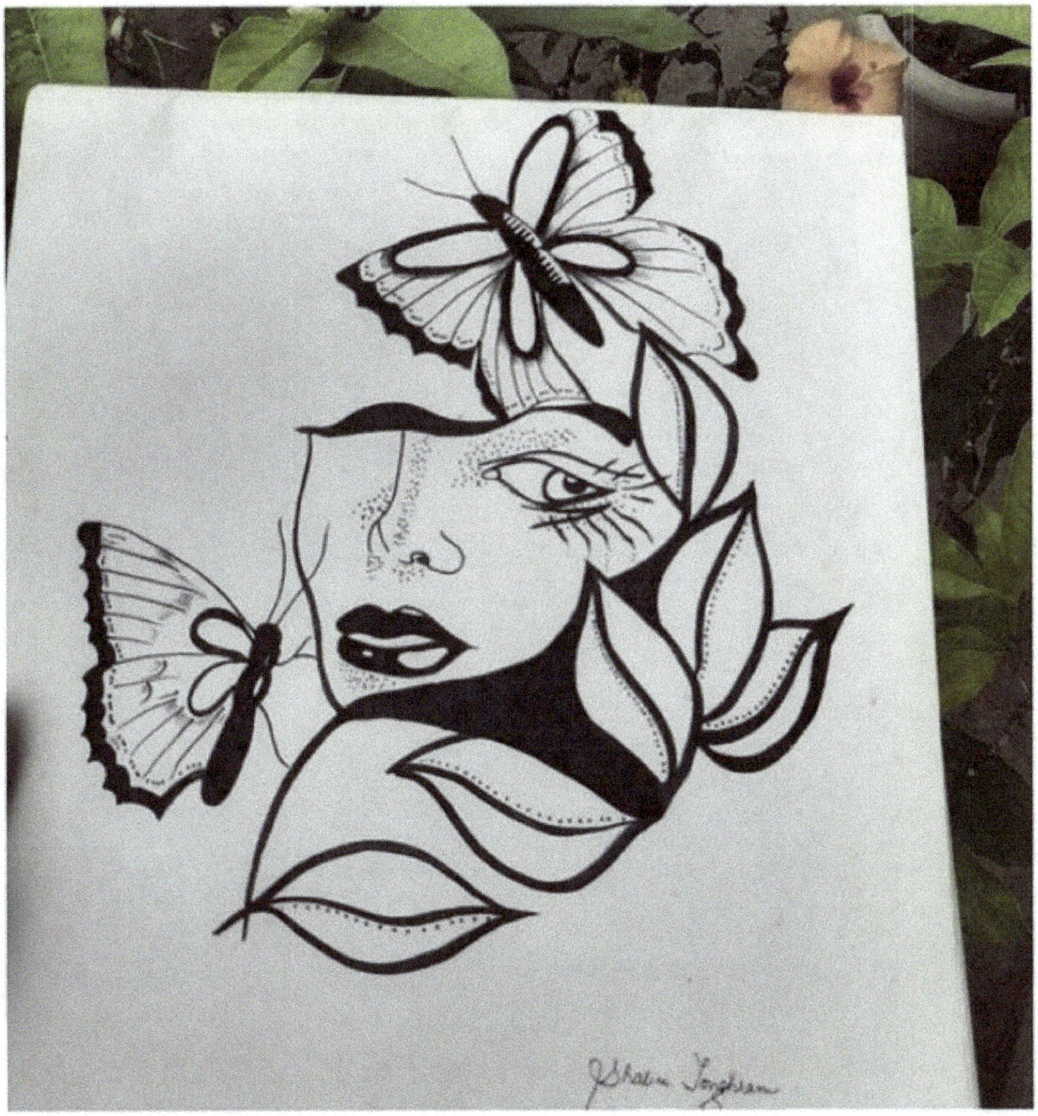

---------*-------

Intentionally Left Blank

---------*-------

ꯁꯨꯃꯇꯤꯔꯕꯦ ꯅꯪ

ꯑꯅꯔ ꯍꯕꯦꯇꯤꯊ ꯍꯁꯦꯊꯇꯃꯔꯃ

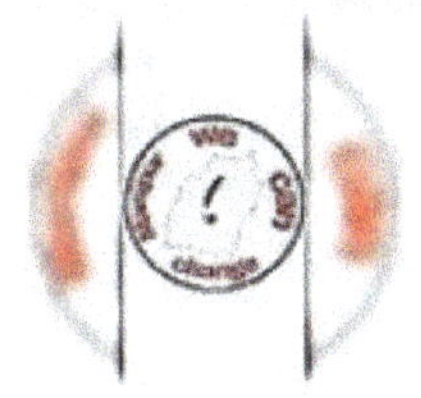

ꯅꯇꯤ ꯊꯪ ꯑ ꯁꯪ ꯑꯇ ꯍꯇꯤ ꯃꯨꯕ

ꯁꯨꯍꯇꯥꯄꯒꯤ ꯅꯣꯡ

ꯑꯃꯥꯍꯄ ꯑꯀ ꯏꯌꯇꯄ
ꯔꯦꯅꯏꯄ ꯈꯥꯔꯦ ꯀꯨꯗꯐꯇꯄ
ꯁꯨꯌ ꯀꯤꯌ ꯂꯨꯌꯥꯔꯪꯌ ꯔꯪꯌꯃꯇ
ꯇꯦꯁꯒꯥ, ꯅꯣꯒꯥ ꯍꯣꯌꯇꯌ ꯈꯥꯔꯦ ꯫
ꯅꯂꯣꯒꯥ ꯅꯣꯒꯌꯏꯍꯃꯥ ꯑꯒꯦꯅꯄꯇꯥ
ꯀꯥꯒꯥ ꯀꯃꯥꯦꯆꯗꯤꯌꯃꯥ ꯏꯇꯄꯃꯥ
ꯊꯦꯁꯒꯪ, ꯃꯦꯍꯇꯪ ꯑꯣꯍꯤꯅꯇ ꯫
ꯃꯪꯆꯃꯄ ꯑꯀꯒꯥ ꯃꯀꯌ
ꯑꯃꯥꯪꯆꯄ ꯇꯥꯂꯥꯌ ꯀꯦꯌꯅꯆꯄ
ꯃꯌꯇꯥꯄꯒꯤ, ꯂꯥꯌꯇꯥꯄꯒꯤ ꯀꯥꯔꯦꯅꯄ ꯫
ꯁꯦꯍꯤ ꯇꯣꯂꯥꯌ ꯑꯒꯪꯍꯄ
ꯑꯃꯌ ꯗꯤꯇꯦ ꯂꯥꯇꯥꯆꯇꯄ
ꯑꯈꯦꯅꯄꯇ ꯈꯤꯌꯥꯅꯇꯥ ꯫
ꯑꯏꯄꯇ ꯁꯣꯌꯇ ꯏꯌꯄꯇꯥ
ꯂꯥꯄ ꯇꯦꯄ ꯔꯦꯁꯒꯂꯨ
ꯍꯤꯌꯇꯌꯃꯨꯒꯥ ꯀꯅꯣꯇꯥ
ꯑꯗꯣꯄꯄꯨ ꯊꯍꯄ ꯑꯂꯥꯄ ꯫
ꯅꯣꯡ ꯅꯣꯂꯪ ꯑꯣꯍꯤꯅ
ꯃꯤꯒꯍ ꯃꯤꯗꯥ ꯑꯒꯦꯅꯄꯇꯥ
ꯃꯨꯇꯃ ꯃꯨꯆꯂꯥ ꯔꯦ ꯔꯦ ꯇꯦꯁꯂꯥ
ꯔꯨꯍꯃ ꯅꯍꯇꯃ ꯇꯦꯍ ꯂꯤꯆꯂꯥ
ꯅꯣꯡ ꯔꯦꯁꯒꯨꯄ ꯂꯨꯌꯊꯦꯅꯪ
ꯅꯔꯪꯌꯃꯥ ꯈꯦꯇꯥꯀꯤꯅ ꯍꯤꯅꯒꯃꯍꯀꯨꯂꯥ꯫
ꯒꯣꯔꯦ ꯒꯦꯍꯃ ꯍꯤꯌꯊꯨꯃ ꯏꯤꯐꯅꯆꯃ
ꯁꯦꯃ ꯁꯤꯀꯦꯒꯥ ꯁꯨꯅꯥ ꯗꯌꯇꯥꯌꯃꯪ
ꯅꯒꯪ ꯈꯨꯒꯥꯂꯇꯇ ꯔꯦꯅꯏꯒꯪ
ꯁꯨꯍꯇꯥꯄꯒꯇꯪ ꯅꯣꯂꯥꯄꯤ ꯁꯦꯃꯤ?

- ꯀꯒꯇꯥꯌ ꯀꯔꯦꯌꯇꯍꯄꯍ

---------*-------

Intentionally Left Blank

---------*-------

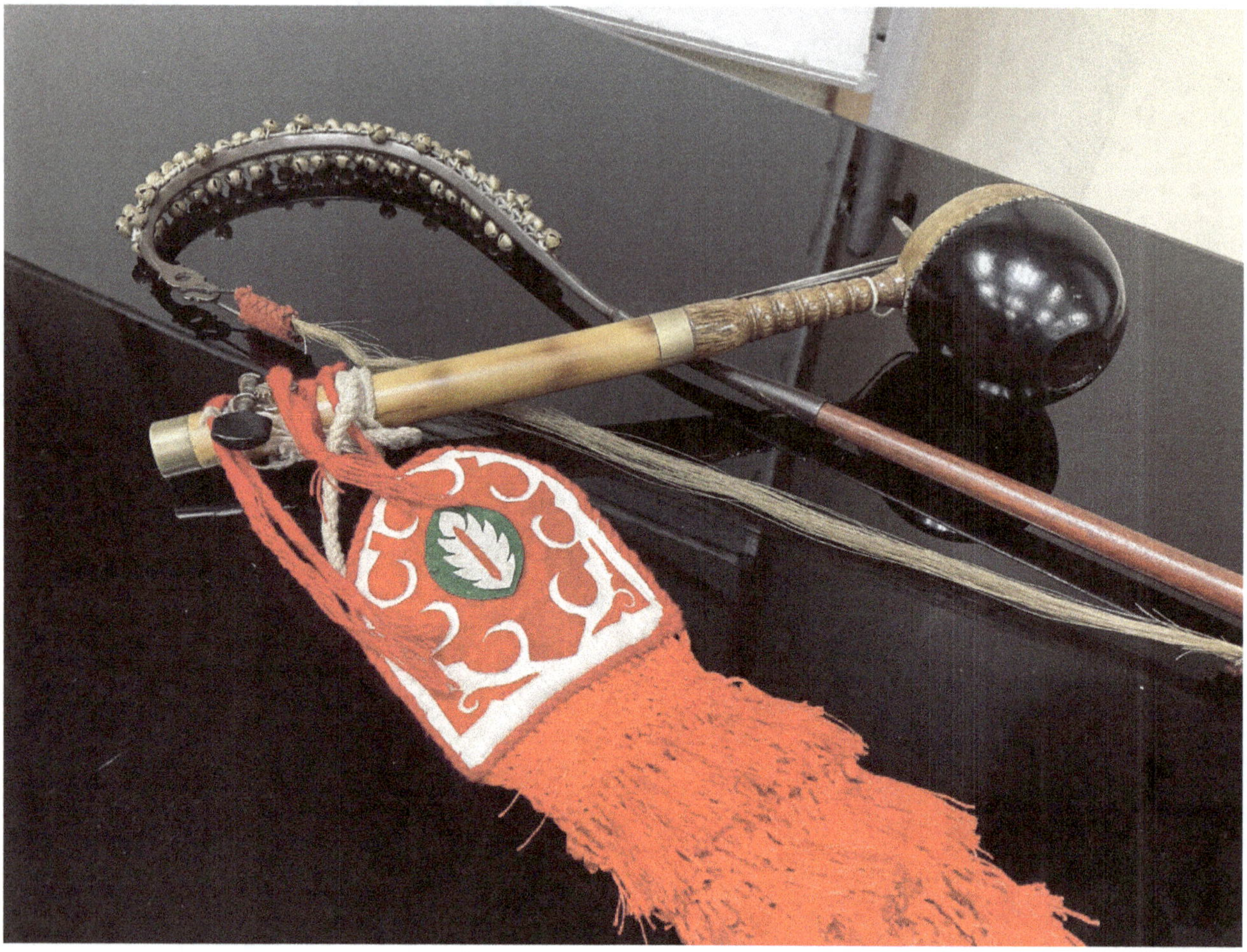

GOAL FIXTURE

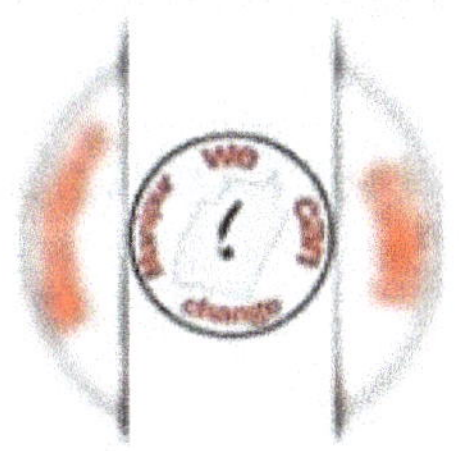

BY NGRISTIN LUKRAM

WE CAN CHANGE MANIPUR-WCCM

Goal Fixture: To dodge these treacherous hurdles, teens need both experienced individuals to provide initial guidance and adequate tools to promote further success.“

by Ngristin Lukram

Goal is a powerful, yet tricky beast. It is really easy to get motivated and find yourself wrapped up in a whirlwind of excitement. But what is the reason behind why you set up your goal?

Goal setting for teens can be daunting: teens have big ideas and big dreams , but don’t yet have the experience of breaking down and organizing a goal into steps. Goals like “Get an A-plus in all of my classes” or “Save enough money for a car” can end in disappointment or abandonment.

If done without planning and intention, a goal could inadvertently hurt a growth mindset. Teens might fail with a vague or lofty goal and then think, "See? I can't do it anyway."

It all depends on one's alternative and heed to what one would like to become when they reach their particular stage. But all should know that "Needs aren't Goals". Most people when questioned define their needs as goals. There is however a distinction between the two. Goals are intended to bring happiness and changing the lifestyle of the individual. On the other hand, self fulfillment is the idea behind needs. Goals should not be set on the basis of needs.

There is great power in self-motivated goals which pertains understanding our priorities and purposes. Difficult as it may be to draw the best priorities from us, it is necessary to maintain our attention to the right 'goals'.

Stake your lives on our goals.

Determination will help us have more motivation seeping into our minds and then into actions, it becomes an esoteric drive that furls us forward. Goals can be either be long term or short term. Again the distinction between these two will vary from one person to another, depending on what the future holds for different people.

Short term goals are often intended to enhance our learning skills or the traits at the particular job, developing ourselves more. They tend to happen in the near future. On the contrary long term goals are related deeply more with our career with our ambitions or maybe settling down or enhancing our lines by including social relevance works. And may take a while before achievements.

Goals therefore are strong elements of self knowledge. As implied earlier aspirations and ambitions are the reasons behind goal setting. They therefore are complimentary; the level of motivation will determine whether they are achieved.

Just think about your own interests 6 or 8 years ago and how different they are from today and you're probably interested in complete different things. Now in 5 or 10 years time, you will be interested in something totally different things again. All these means that your present interests are just not a solid basis on which to choose a career.

Let's throw some light on the problems faced by education system in India.

1.Lack of Guidance at Home: Nobody is able to solve the problems in their studies at home as other members of family are busy too. In that case they have to rely largely on guidance at school.

2. Academic Stress, Parental Pressure, Anxiety and Mental Health among Students: Academic stress involves mental distress regarding anticipated academic challenges or failure or even an awareness of the possibility of academic failure. Parent pressure is when a parent puts too much strain on their child to force them to exceed.

The pressure is normally to be the best in the chosen field, even one that they used to succeed at and now can't. In a study conducted on 190 students from grade 11 to 12 from 3 private schools in Kolkata and 3 government-aided schools, it was found out that almost two-thirds of the students experienced pressure from their parents to perform better academically.

3.Exams and subjects: Examinations are more focused on end results, rather than continuous learning. Most subjects, for example, science and material science, center around course reading information, when they could be fun applied subjects to learn.

4.And a Drawback of the New Education Policy: In the National Education Policy 2020, language is a negative factor as there is a problematic teacher to student ratio in India, thus introducing mother languages for each subject in academic institutes is a problem.

Sometimes, finding a competent teacher becomes a problem and now another challenge comes with the introduction of the NEP 2020, that is bringing study material in mother languages.

5. Expenses: Numerous schools charge extravagant expenses, which turns into a weight for guardians. Schools with moderate expenses for the most part have lesser assets, which influence the nature of training.

6. And Et cetera

So these are needed to be done in to help them

1. More Accountability

2. Removing psychological bias towards them,

3. Benefits of New Education Policy 2020

Some of the important benefits of the New Education Policy 2020 are as follows:

The New Education Policy will give importance to students' practical knowledge instead of just pushing them towards rote learning.

It will help students to develop scientific temper from a young age. The NEP aims to make it easier to set up new quality of higher educational institutes which will be at par with the global standards. Since NEP will make it easier for foreign colleges to set up the campuses here many students who are unable to go abroad due to multiple reasons will be able to experience it and get global

4. Encouragement through scholarships

5. Focus on your Needs aren't your goals too

We are confused yes! Yes we are. Goal setting for the current generation has been a problem for the current generation. Why is it difficult for us to have clearly set goals? Despite the fact that there are 1.8 billion young people between the ages 10 and 24 in the world, the daily routines cannot make us make decisions on what we want to achieve. The routines are complicated beyond our understanding. So how can we encounter this? The answer is clear, understand your routines. Set your priorities right.

The University of Oxford did 3 years of research centered on the career to goals and concluded that most people have lost focus in terms of choosing the right career. This has consequently led to alteration of an individual's ambition since they can focus on a goal different from the career, all the research and thinking has led us to the conclusion that career advice today focuses on the wrong thing. Throughout most of history people basically did what their parents told them to. Some people in the 1980s were driven by the slogan "The Greed is Good" and focused on making money. The current generation has however grown up with some different career advices and that's "that you should follow your passion". Unfortunately, the 'passion' is decided and directed by the parents and society. The only remedy to for this is to break from the bondage of limited decisions and stop fulfilling the expectations of the society. Rather, we ought to deeply scrutinise our heart, fathom our own desires and start chasing our dreams.

Well you need to follow these three steps to satisfy your internal motives.

-identify your greatest interests,

-find careers that match those interests and

-pursue those careers no matter what!

But think about it in a bit more depth, turns out if you follow your passion and make a single wrong move, you're probable going to fail. Dreams are prone to become invalid, so does the goals. The reason behind this is probably that during our ages, we had unrealistic desires. On the contrary, the desires might have been realistic but due to prevailing economic, social and cultural conditions, we are forced to shift from our dreams. Further outside influence could be a contributing factor.

A recent survey on students reveals 90% of them were passionate about sports, art, music. However the census data showed that only 3% of jobs are covered in these fields. This implies that as much as individuals are willing to chase their dream, the industry does not fully accommodate their ambitions.

So it just has to be the case that even if only one in ten people followed their passion. Still the majority would fail to be successful.

---------*-------

Intentionally Left Blank

---------*-------

HAPPINESS

BY LUMREICHAN NK

WE CAN CHANGE MANIPUR-WCCM

wccm2024 'HAPPINESS'

Happiness can be in many forms. It can mean different
things to different people.
For me, Happiness is accepting who you are as a person,
regardless of your flaws and not comparing yourself with
anyone else.
Happiness is being grateful for the little things you have in
life and not wanting for more.
Happiness is being able to let go off the past and learn
from the mistakes.
Happiness is accepting that you do not have control over
the words and actions of others, and what they say about
you does not define who you are as a person.

Happiness is in doing things that you believe is right and
just, without fear of judgment.
Finally, happiness is in being there for people who need
you.
And if one day, I forget all these and I am consumed by
misery and sadness, remind me that I once was happy and
I can be happy again. Remind me that time heals all
wounds.

– Lumreichan NK

#wecanchangemanipur

12 June 2021

----------*-------

Intentionally Left Blank

----------*-------

IN THE NAME OF LOVE

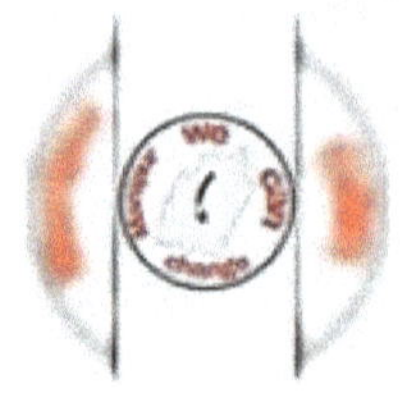

BY ROTIKA HAOBAM

WE CAN CHANGE MANIPUR-WCCM

wccm2024 'In The Name Of Love'

In the name of Love
You come into my life
In the name of love
You walk away....
What an irony is it...
But it leave a deep scar
In my Heart
In the name of Love
In the name of Love
Everything is beautiful, lovely, dreams.
In the name of Love
Everything becomes dull, hopeless,
scary dreams.
Nostalgic memory arises in eyes
Only in the name of Love...
Tears keep falling down...

– Rotika Haobam
(RJ7).

#wecanchangemanipur

19 June 2021

---------*-------

Intentionally Left Blank

---------*-------

INDIA HANDLING OF COVID 19 PANDEMIC

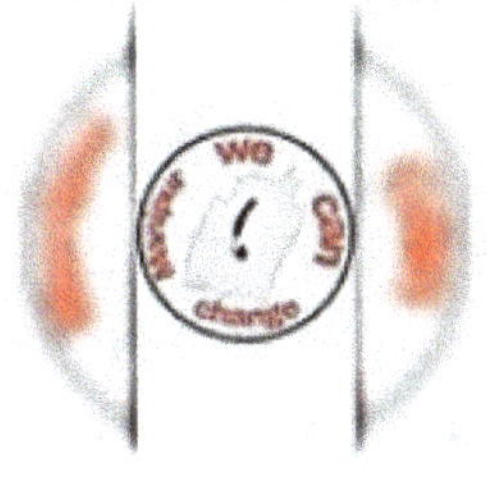

BY KONSAM KELVIN

WE CAN CHANGE MANIPUR-WCCM

'India Handling Of Covid 19 Pandemic'

By Konsam Kevin

India is going through the worst phase of the pandemic. The rapid surge of covid 19 cases in India from the third week of February is a major source of concern for public, government, health care workers, etc. reaching an all time high of 4 lakhs new covid-19 case. The states of Maharashtra, Kerala, Uttar Pradesh, Delhi and Karnataka continue to be the worst hit state and have contributed most to the rising cases of Coronavirus in India.

Earlier, at the end of first wave 60 pc of population has been affected by the virus. The uninfected percent may be 40 pc of the whole population. according to the recent Indian council of medical research report, the reinfection rate in India stands at 4.5 pc.

The current pace of vaccination and two weeks interval required after second dose of vaccine to confer sufficient immunity to decelerate second wave indicate that vaccine alone can't help in curving the pandemic

Country faced many challenges in controlling its virus— India being second largest population in the world, socially diverse country comprising of both very rural areas and crowded urban area.

one of the remarkable government strategies in controlling the virus is by unveiling vaccine strategy

1) the phase rolled out of vaccination drive initiated on January 16 under which vaccine eligible section of population were gradually increased and has been extended to entire adult population- those above 18 years of age.

2) vaccine manufacture now has a freedom to sell 50pc of their production to the state and private hospitals.

the phase rolled out of vaccination drive beginning with health care and frontline workers in January followed by inclusion of people above 45 years of age in march and April respectively.

This pandemic has devastated people livelihood and causes tremendous downfall in the Indian economy, rise in unemployment, collapse of tourism and hospitality industry, GDP contraction.

The government should focus on the vaccination drive rather than imposing lockdown or so to say curfew in almost all the states of the country except in the few states where it has gone out of hand.

India should increase its testing rates several times over and it should be made priority for the government.

Given the crowd of India and high rate of infection universal make wearing with high quality mask should be made mandatory.

Banning of all indoor and outdoor events, religious gathering, rallies, weeding and so on is a must.

At the same time, government has faced many criticisms in controlling the pandemic. Irrespective of your thought, believes, association the country should be united in fighting and in overcoming this pandemic as one person rather targeting the government and destroying Indian image globally and defaming the prime minister.

---------*-------

Intentionally Left Blank

---------*-------

ꯃꯩꯇꯂꯥꯀꯌꯥꯊꯥ

ꯍꯅꯊꯥ ꯁꯤꯀꯈꯥꯄꯪꯕ ꯅꯦꯅꯕꯧꯎꯔꯛꯆ

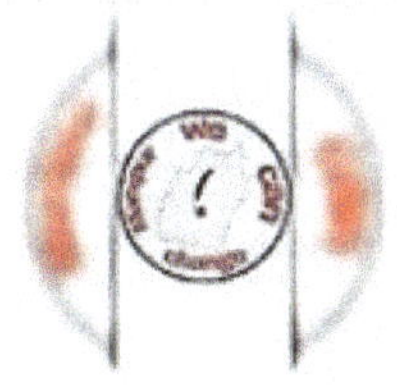

ꯌꯥ ꯃꯪꯉ ꯁꯪꯉꯂ ꯈꯇꯥꯔꯨꯕꯧ

[illegible]

[illegible]

- [illegible]

---------*-------

Intentionally Left Blank

---------*-------

KAREMNABIRI

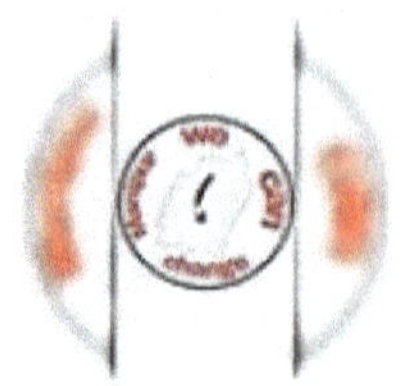

BY SOUGAIJAM LEINGAKLEMBI

WE CAN CHANGE MANIPUR-WCCM

wccm2024 'Karemnabiri'

Torbangi khonglam machasidi
Yaanganglabi echelgi tunginduna
Lengdana mahoushagum leiramli
Chingsilli eibu manakta.
Ningamdana houkhraba warina
Pareng pareng chatlamli
Cheikhei chingkhraba thoudoksingna
Yachanglakpasida nouhounarakli.
Akangba unana kellakpada
Magi khongthangni khalluri
Kouning nayengluba maikeiduda
Liraba upal duna karemnabiri.

–Sougaijam Leingaklembi

View 1 comment

5 June 2021 • See translation

---------*-------

Intentionally Left Blank

---------*-------

ꯃꯨꯅꯀꯣꯕꯧ

ꯄ ꯍ ꯀ ꯏꯤ ꯕꯤ ꯋ ꯄꯦ ꯕ ꯍꯪ

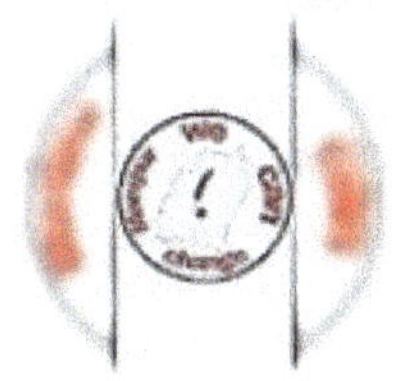

ꯖꯤ ꯍꯪ ꯅ ꯆꯪ ꯅ ꯇ ꯈ ꯂꯤ ꯊꯨ ꯕ

ꯈꯨꯗꯣꯡꯕꯩ

ꯂꯤꯆꯥꯡ ꯇꯥꯡꯖꯥꯗꯤ ꯊꯥꯡꯒꯠ ꯇꯩꯕꯤꯅꯤ
ꯇꯩꯕꯣꯌ ꯇꯥꯡꯖꯥꯗꯤ ꯊꯥꯡꯒꯠ ꯐꯣꯡꯕꯤꯅꯤ
ꯇꯩꯕꯣꯌ ꯇꯩꯆꯠꯂꯤ ꯇꯩꯈꯣꯡ ꯑꯣꯇꯦꯒꯤꯅꯤ
ꯍꯪꯆꯤꯌꯐꯦꯝ ꯁꯪꯌꯇꯩ ꯁꯨꯅ ꯇꯩ
ꯑꯣꯇꯪꯃ-ꯑꯣꯗꯐꯩ ꯀꯨꯞꯇ ꯇꯩ
ꯍꯅꯨꯌ-ꯍꯑꯣꯕꯨꯁꯦ ꯈꯣꯡꯗꯇ ꯇꯩ
ꯆꯨꯕꯦ ꯑꯣꯇꯥꯦ ꯑꯣꯗꯨꯇ ꯇꯩ
ꯆꯨꯌꯂꯤ ꯈꯤꯂꯤ ꯌꯦꯗꯇ ꯇꯩ
ꯆꯤꯌꯆꯦꯟ ꯍꯊꯨꯞꯂꯤꯗꯨꯇ, ꯆꯨꯌꯂꯤ ꯑꯣꯇꯁꯃ ꯇꯩ
ꯈꯅꯦꯒꯤ ꯍꯪꯀꯨꯃ ꯆꯍꯤꯅꯇ, ꯁꯥꯅꯤ ꯇꯕꯦꯌ ꯐꯌꯇꯕꯒꯥ
ꯇꯩꯂꯦ-ꯇꯩꯊꯟ ꯆꯦꯗꯇ ꯇꯪꯌꯇꯒꯥ
ꯊꯨꯌꯇꯒꯥ ꯆꯩꯂꯤ ꯊꯌꯂꯃꯃꯨꯃ
ꯇꯩꯑꯣꯨꯟ ꯌꯦꯗꯇ ꯂꯪꯃꯇꯒꯥ ꯍꯤꯗꯇ ꯌꯦꯗꯅ ꯆꯈꯣꯝ

- ꯒꯤꯕꯤꯂꯦ ꯌꯦꯕ ꯈꯪ

---------*-------

Intentionally Left Blank

---------*-------

LINE LESS ONLINE CLASSES, FOODLESS BILLIONAIRES

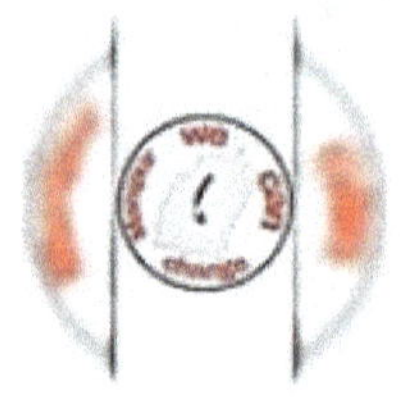

BY NANCY B'KHURAIJAM

WE CAN CHANGE MANIPUR-WCCM

"Line less online classes , foodless billionaires"

by Nancy B'Khuraijam

According to the government instructions , the schools and other higher institutions are conducting online classes . It is the government's high time to know that some people can't afford to buy smartphones for their children to study and to attend online classes . Adding to that some are dying due to lack of medical facilities to treat their previous illnesses or covid related illness . On the other side the government think that our people are lack of food supply and hence make an effort to distribute rice and pulses under NFSA . As a citizen I think our honourable Prime Minister Sir Narendra Modi (I won't say "ji" as I'm a Meitei from Manipur) has already announced the free distribution of rice for the month of May and June under NFSA but in contrast we the citizen have to buy the rice for Rs 3 per Kg . I would not ask why but how? As a vigilant citizen I would like to question our government and to make known that at this difficult situation of pandemic some people are not affordable to buy the rations at the said price and some others can . As a student I feel the urge to let the government open both eyes for these concerns and to make themselves more responsible, accountable and transparent to the citizens and to see people equally and provide according to the needs .

So lastly "If you see peoples equally, then provide equally".

---------*-------

Intentionally Left Blank

---------*-------

MENTAL BREAKDOWN AMIDST THE HOUSE ARREST DURING COVID PANDEMIC

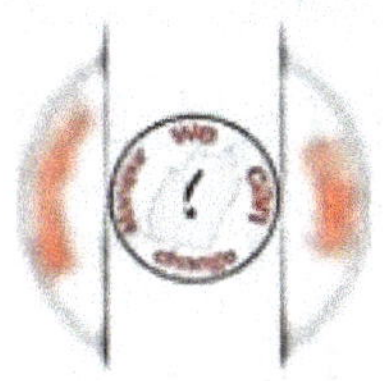

BY ANDREW TAYENJAM

WE CAN CHANGE MANIPUR-WCCM

'Mental breakdown Amidst the House Arrest During Covid Pandemic'

by Andrew Tayenjam

With the prevailing situation of the Covid-19, the state government has imposed an order of total lockdown where everyone has compelled to confined to their house itself. And by living our life single handedly (house arrest) for frequent days, without intermingling with the outside environment, life has now become a monotonous one where there is no fresh and productive mind at all. There has been no room for social gathering, exposure, went for work and so on. And as a result there tend to rise an issue of mental breakdown with the house arrest being the core reason.

When we confined in a house for a long period of time and being apart from realty and outside world, the level of imagination and fantasy gets high and intense leading to the uncontrolled state of mind. And past painful incidents as a flashback do came sometimes in which it leads to hesitation and toxic of mind. And due to the lockdown, most of the people (especially the youths) engaged themselves more in social media. It too affects the mental health subconsciously.

As the coronavirus pandemic rapidly sweeps across the world, it thus induces a considerable degree of fear, anxiety, depression, worry and concern in the population at large and among certain groups in particular, such as adults, care providers and people with underlying health conditions.

Some major principles to reduce stress during the pandemic;

Regular exercise can still be done for our mental health. It plays a vital role in elevating our mood and keeping a positive attitude and keeps our mind calm.

And here we can cite one measure, i.e. engaging ourselves at productive and useful things and which we are more skilled and inclined to, such as gardening, singing, dancing, writing, reading and so on. It diverts our mind from the redundant site and thus creates our creativity itself.

During these times of uncertainty, it is essential to connect other especially with our family members, instead of keeping intact ourselves with the electronic devices which we keeps on scrolling unnecessary posts.

Very importantly, we should always find ways to express our feeling and thoughts and emotions(the stirred or moved up state of our own self) by putting pen to paper, conversation with our nearest ones etc.

And last but not the least, "Meditation" which helps to stop our mind from rushing about in an aimless stream of thoughts.

---------*-------

Intentionally Left Blank

---------*-------

ꯀꯤꯊꯝ ꯂꯣꯃꯆꯣ
ꯊꯤꯇꯩꯁꯦ

ꯑꯍꯔ ꯑꯆꯤꯌꯦꯅꯕ ꯆꯣꯃꯀꯩꯊꯝꯀ

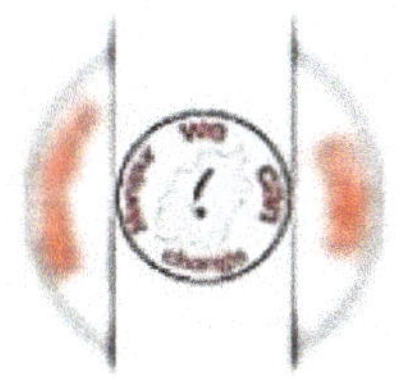

ꯁꯤ ꯊꯪ ꯁꯪ ꯀꯆꯤꯝꯕ

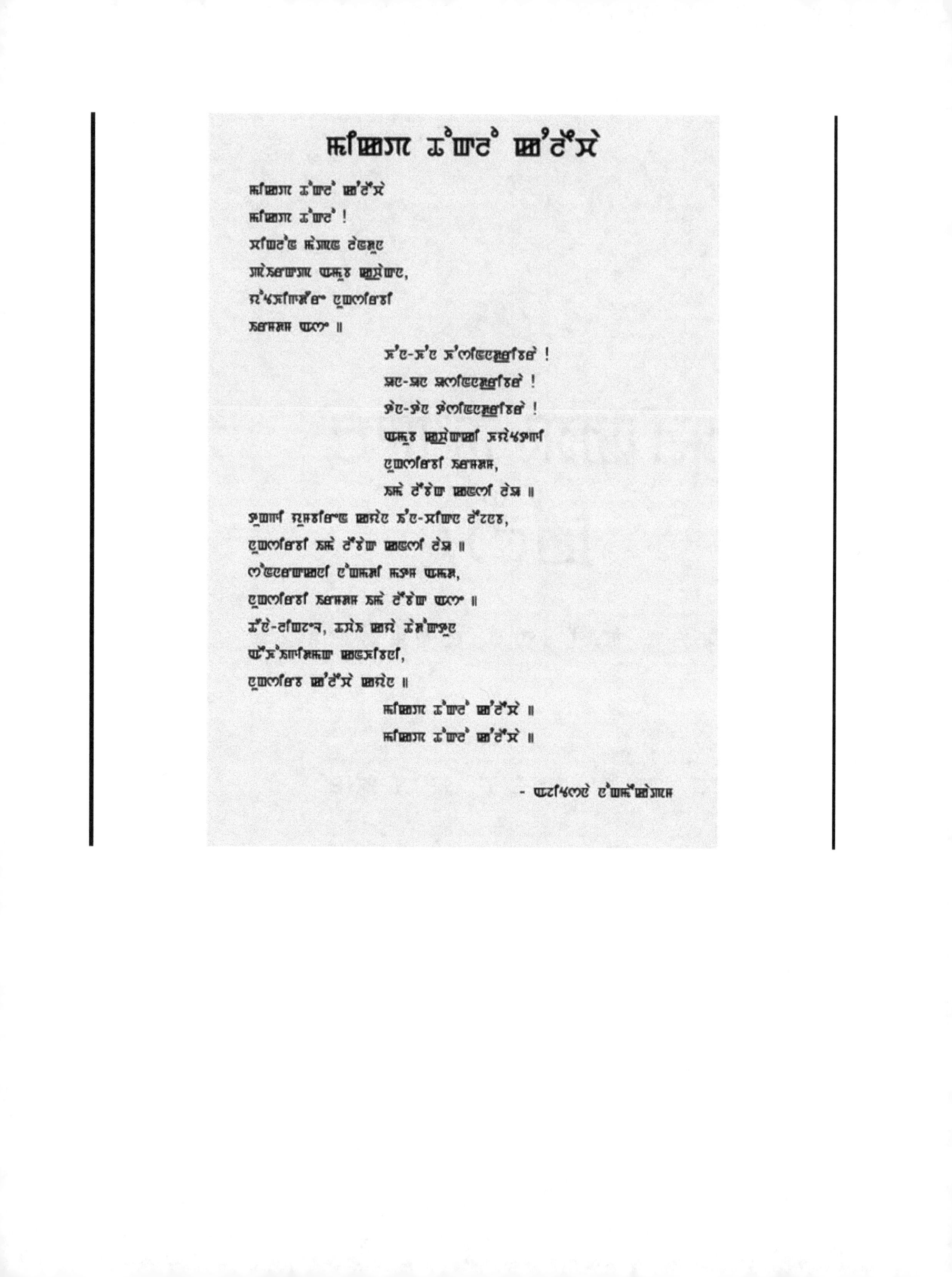

[illegible]

[illegible]
[illegible] !
[illegible]
[illegible],
[illegible]
[illegible] ॥

[illegible] !
[illegible] !
[illegible] !
[illegible]
[illegible],
[illegible] ॥

[illegible],
[illegible] ॥
[illegible],
[illegible] ॥
[illegible], [illegible]
[illegible],
[illegible] ॥

[illegible] ॥
[illegible] ॥

- [illegible]

---------*-------

Intentionally Left Blank

---------*-------

NATIONAL EDUCATION POLICY 2020 AMASUNG SEX EDUCATION GI MARUOIBA

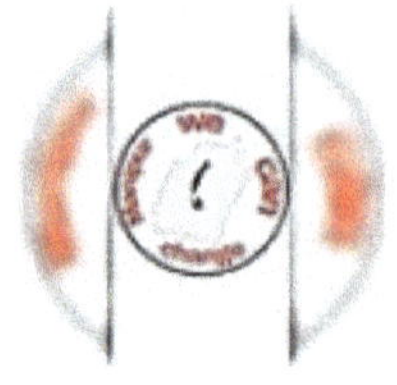

BY NAMEIRAKPAM SEIROWNA CHANU

WE CAN CHANGE MANIPUR-WCCM

National Education Policy 2020 amasung Sex Education gi Maruoiba

by Nameirakpam Seirowna Chanu

Leibak amgi apunba fivam ama honghanbada amsung pandam ama fangnaba hotnabda education gi yamna chaorba thoudang lei. Masigidamk mtm gi mtung enna leibak adugi Education curriculum semdok semjin twba darkar lei. Bharat ki apunba meeshing asi China gi hek mthngda yamba anisubani amsung leppa leitana hengtlkli. Yamlaba Mishing asigi manungda adolescences haibdi chahi 10 dgi 19 faobgi mnungda leiba miyoisingnaa chada 21 oiri. Amaromda leibak asida thokliba sex-related crimes, chahi nwriba angangsingda chthba molestation, rape nachingba thoudok kaya asukki mtik chang wangle. Pumnamk asi yenglaga eikhoigi Education curriculum da ahongba khra purkpa yarabara haibdu khnnba mtm ywre. Handkta nwna fongkhiba National Education Policy 2020 "Sex Education" ga mari leinaba hiram macha khaina uba fngdba asimk laibak thibani. Sok 1968 tagi leirkkhiba Education Policy asi Sok 1986 amsung sok 1992 da ahongba kaya thokhrbasu ngasifaba Sex Education da emphasis piba leitri. "Online" amsung "Digital" haiba waheising asi yam toina uba fnglabasu yaofm thokpa mru oiba topic ama chithhrmba asina 21st century da mityeng thmba Policy asigi wahnthok mpung fahndre. Mtm kuindgi dharma sanskriti ki mrumda lottuna leirurba sex education gi hiram asi eikhoi punna fongna khnna neinaba mtm ywre.

Sex Education gi matangda mkha neindringeida masina kari hairibano amsung topic asina kadaifaoba konbage haibdu khngminnsi. Hairiba hiram asina eikhoida mioibgi sex (nupi nupa oibgi shkwong takliba) amsung sexuality gi mrm da gyan lwshing pi. Masida nttna eikhoigi sexual anatomy amsung thwongsing ,finunggi hksel, masiga mari leinaba adhikar nachingba kaya amasu khnghnli. Msina mi amgi masa da thokpa amsung atoppa gendera da thokpa hkchangi ahongba kayagi mrmda gyan tahnli. Malemgi mfm kayada Sex Education na kannba kaya pirabsu eikhoigi leibak asidadi hujiksu yetnaningai oirba topic ama oiri. Sok 2005 ta sarkarna Ministry of Human Resource Development (MHRD) amsung NACO(National AIDS Control Organisation)ga khutsmnaduna Adolescence Education Programme laothkhiba mtmda bharat ta leiriba State 13 na program asi athingba thmkhi. Houjik biology syllabusta yaoriba reproduction gi saruk amsung school singda mtm mtm gi mtung enna pangthokpa programme kaya asina mpung faba sex education ni haibdudi langani. Masida hakchanggi, pukninggi, wakhl gi oiba enkhtlkliba naha singna khngdba yadba lwsing gyan kaya ama chithhari. Khudam ama nupisingna Contraceptive Pills chaba yai khnglabsu masigi side effects, amangba kaya gi mrmda mpung fana khngnade. Msidgi fttba kaya thokhnbada nttna suicide twba faoba twb wakhlfaoba khlhnli. Leikai da samaj ta sex educationgi mrmda ngasifaobda da fongna ngangnade amsung masigi mrmda ngangnabsingbu aranba mityengda yengbi. Atoppa khudam amada houjik houjik eikhoina fongna uba fngba hairgadi nupisingna yum pallba mtungda manem-mku singna angang nupa poktangi otpi neibiba emung khrdadi thokli. Masi Sex education gi mngal fngdabdgi. Mtm kuindgi hiram asi eikhoi gi chtnabi dharmagi mayoktani amsung msina nahasingda fttba wakhl, thouwong kaya ama thokhnli haib thajabsina nmhttuna lakli. Samajgi maikei khudingdagi- ahn lmn, dharmagi akhng aheising, shkti leiba rajniti wala singdgi athingba kaya ama thmduna lake e.

Amromda eikhoidi snskriti ngakna chtchba kanglupni, asigumba mhei lousing mthou tade haina mioi khrandi chaothokpa pokchei. Miyoibagi hakchangda mhousana chahi mtanggi gi mtung enna ahongba thok ee twbtabu masibu eikhoina lotsinduna thmjnli, kanagasu masigi mtangda fongna wari sannde. Kanagumba amana puberty ywrba mtmda honglklib kaya asi gyan ningthina leitbdgi masabu hnthana khnjba, wakhl piksinb, masidgi hendoktuna mental health ta faoba sokhnlkpa yaowee. Nupi mchasingna ekaiba kaya leibana thokliba ahongbsing lotsinnba hotnbada awaba kaya thengnei. Eikhoina samasya sing asi atei atoppa hiram neinbgum neinde. Sex education asibu luna lwriba leibak mayam gi mnungda the Netherlands su amani. Leibak asida Teen birth haibdi nouriba nupisingna angang unnbgi changsi yamna hnthana uba fngee. Houjikki mtmda chahi nouriba angang singna yamna laina internet, magazines amsung atei lmbisingdgi sex ki mrmda yengba,paba fngi twbatabu madudagi fnglkpa e-pao adu aranba amsung lanna lmjingba yaba kaya ama yaowee. Mrm asina sex education gi mrmda mrik chumba pao piba ngmba education curiiculum ama leifm thoktabara haibsini. Nongma Kangdana tattana thokliba chahi nouriba (minor) singda chtthba sex crimes aduga asigumba crime kayada juvenile na saruk yaba pumnamk asi urga eikhoi karigumba khrdi twfm thok ee. Nibhaya Case ta court na rai pikhiba maruoiba culprit adu juvenile ni. Masidasu nttna machanupi minor ani apokpa mapana tha kaya sexual abuse twduna thmbirmbgi thoudoksu leiri. Masi khudm khrkhk lwkhtchbni. Houjik Houjik eikhoina article asi paringeida emung amada asigumba sexual abuse, molestation nachingba kaya chtthrmloi hainingai leite.

Sex Education tmbagi kannaba asi asukki mtik yamkhre. Eikhoina masigi mrmda tmbibana nahasingbu aranba lmbida lmjinggni haiba asi hiram asigi mrmda munna khngdbadgini. Sex Education na atenba mtm da piba yaba kannabadgi hwrga tung koina samaj ki oiba apunba afba purkpada mteng panggni. Kannbsing smlma thmlabada :

--- masina nahasingda puberty mtmda thokpa hakchanggi amsung wakhl gi oiba ahongba kaya gi mrmda vap tahnli

--- finunggi hksel (Sexual health) amsung luba nanba (hygiene), leina sndokoidba mwonggi sex practices ki mrm khnghnli

--- HIV/AIDS tagi ngakthokpa amsung ngangthokpa sndokpa thingba amsung loina loinana STDs singdagi cheksinhnli

--- nupi amda mirondringei mamang amsung mirollba mtungda lwhtkdba cheksin thourang sing gi mrmda khngli

--- pamdaba mironba thingnaba pambei sing, family planning gi lwsing amsung meeshing henglkpa thingbada chaona mteng pangi

--- mi amagi ayaba lwba amsung apam pamdgi wakhllon adubu ekaikhumnaba, partner anigi mrkta leinba mrigi mrmda tak ee

--- sexual abuse tagi esa ngakthoknaba lwsing gyan pi

--- nouna angang unnba , mama amsung mcha sibagi chang hnthahnnbada thoudang lwee.

Eikhoina Sex education gi kannba kaya ama khngalabsu hiram asibu hnggoiba ekaiba yaodna masigi mrmda khnna neinaba ngmlagdra haiba wahng amdi leiri. Syllabus ta haplabsu masibu ningthina chtnahnbadi miyam pumnamkki thoudangni. Mama Mapadgi hwraga, satra , oja, mayam punna hotnminnba mthou tai. Subject asi heindbgi khudam oina hairgdi Oja singna reproduction gi para ywrkpada ekaibdgi takpidba amsung exam nachingbadsu para adudgi wahng hngdaba kaya asi hujik hujiksu thokli. Satrsingnasu ekaibadgi nttrga satra ateina lknrkkni kibdgi khngningba kaya hngdana tuminn leisnli. Masi ojagi Training amsung awareness watpadagini. Sarkar gi maikeidagi mtm mtm gi channba sex ed training pifm thok ee, school amana oja lwba mtmdasu subject sigi takpa ngmgdba oja khnbiba mthou tai. Yumdasu mama mapasingna machasingda school da tmmiba para adugi akhng khngdbni. Satrsingnasu yumda mahakki mchil mnao amsung emung mnungda sex ed ki mtangda khnna neinba yai.

---------*-------

Intentionally Left Blank

---------*-------

NUPA NA KHUTLINGBA SAMAJ DA "NUPA"

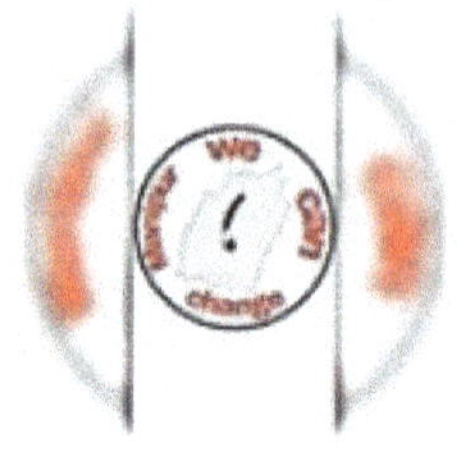

BY SUSHITRA KHOIROM

WE CAN CHANGE MANIPUR-WCCM

Nupana khutlingba samaj da 'NUPA'

by Sushitra Khoirom

Ngasi oiriba Manipur samaj asi nupana khutlingba samaj amani haina eikhoi pumnamakna lounari. Thouna farabi nupi kayana nupa ga nupi ga right mannahangadabani haina akanba khollao laoduna akanba khongjang changsilli. Adubu nupasu 'chatnabi' haiba waheisina makhong makhut punsinduna lengba otpa ngamdana leiba yaodabadi natte. Chatnabi haibasi karino, kanana karamba matamdagi houdoklambano? Masidi eikhoi meeoibana eikhoi esagidamak semjabani. Esana thajaba chara, makhong somduna esing chaiduna wana semjarakpa, nupa nupagi khennaba leitrba saktam amakhakni. Nupa khaktana thakhiba nupi khaktana esing chaiduna makhong somduna semkhiba ntte. Aduga karigino ekhutna thajakhiba pambidudagi uhei amafaoba pat thatlaga chaba kijariba. Samaj asigi chatnabibu semkhiba meeoiba eikhoina chatnabi mabu asuk kiruriba karigino?

Nupi kayana pendana phongdokli, "Emung manung gi thabak makup mata su eikhoina touba, angang sennabasu eikhoina, waisit wairm su eikhoina. Nupa makhoidi mapan thoklaga sel tanbasikhak nattradi atei emung gi thabak khajiktang mateng pangsinbirakpa yadabra?" Matang asida taseng tasengnamak eihakki emitsina uba enasina tajrkpa meeoi anikhakki wari matek amamamta lijrkke. Ahanbada, private school gi oja oibi meeyai challabi nupi amna chahi naha oiriba nupa amda cheirambagi warini. Nupa asi numit khuding gi thabk hallakpada pikliba machanupa bu "Papa gi Thoithoiba" haina kouduna hek hek changlak e. Nupi aduna naha aduda cheirk e "ahal laman leiriba mayamsigi mamangda namaido karimta ekaidabra" Nupi ase atei kanasu natte naha asigi lairik laisu heirabi mamani. Nupa asi thabakta chilhao thiba misak natte.

Magi nupina emung gi thabak enkhang hotnaduna leirabsu machabu chak hek pijabiba, eru hek luthokpiba angamba mateng hekta pangsillk e. Adugisu nupi gi mathou nupagi mathou khangde hekta haibi. School dadi satrasingda taklamgani "nupa na nupi bu ekai khumnaba, women empowerment haibasi yumdagi hanna tamgadabani". Anisuba wari asina leibakki fam achouba pairiba nupa amagi warini. Macha ningol ngakta ani pok e . Macha nupi atonbido pammaga lambida chathoubado ubada meeyam na ngangnei "masigi nupa asina touriba asibu mamannaba ukhraga magi ejat sibu kaidano. Nupisu nattaba nupa, adugisu mathakta officer mana touja sajarisibu keino? Nupa di macha nungsiba yadabra? Nupana mapan thokna macha nungsiba utpa yade haibasibu karamba samaj ki karamba chatnabino? Migi mapot maral huralluba natte. Masida ekainingai, thina ngangnaningai leite. Asigumba chaokhatningai wakhal chenba nupasing asibu hanthana yengbirabadi nupibu minaigum sijinnaba fadi sabamakhei sumba nupasing adudi thak wangna thagatkadra?

Asumna cheibiba, noknabibagi mahutta makhoibu thagat wahei kharadang phongdokpirabadi yumthong yumthong gi nupasingdasu wakhal lousing oigadabani. Aphaba chaokhatpagi apunba masak ama semba ngamgani.

Kadomdano mapangal kallaba nupasing asina thagadaba makhongsibo? Samaj asibu kinabu chatkadra, nupi mayamna changsilliba 'women empowerment' gi khongjang asibu support tougadra?Samaj gi minok meisa langlibasi nupi khaktadara? Natte, nupasuni. Karamba matamda nupa- nupi mannana leiba khunai ama oirakkani? Ngasi nupi eikhoina nupa gi mkhada leiriba karigino? Nupina sonthana leiribasi kanagi maral no, nupasing gi maral la nattraga minok chaoba noknagadoubagi maya kaduna leiraba samaj asigi maral la? Mayam punna khanminnasi.

---------*-------

Intentionally Left Blank

---------*-------

OH THE EDGY

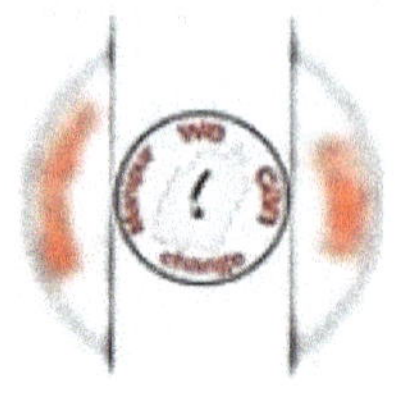

BY WUSHAKPHY MUINAO

WE CAN CHANGE MANIPUR-WCCM

wccm2024 'Oh The Edgy'

New day comes another headlines
Of pandemic as just as fair.
They and I
Doubted deadlines for ourselves,
With a sigh!
Oh the edgy!
Sennight comes around again
Thy mystifying apathy comes.
They and I
Grin like a cheshire cat,
Weep underneath.
Oh the edgy!
Quick as wink;
Like clockwork.
They and I
Goes on in due course.
Surely but slowly far flung
will sail by coast to coast
Oh the edgy.

– Wushakphy Muinao

#wecanchangemanipur

12 June 2021

---------*-------

Intentionally Left Blank

---------*-------

ERA OF COVID: LIFE AND EDUCATION

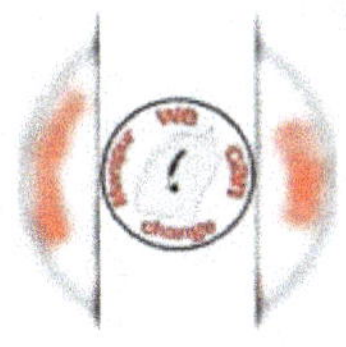

BY POTSHANGBAM SUSHMA DEVI

WE CAN CHANGE MANIPUR-WCCM

ERA OF COVID: LIFE AND EDUCATION

by Potshangbam Sushma Devi

Who could have ever thought that the new normal among the socially dependent species like humans would-be social distancing? That the trending fashion or 'popular' item would be face masks and sanitizers? Who would have thought cleanliness and good hygiene would play such a crucial role in keeping a tab on this deadly pandemic that's eating away and sucking the soul out of daily life? If we had been taught in our school days just a few years back that the simple act of washing hands could save humanity, we would have probably laughed it off as mere exaggeration. But unfortunately, nothing is predictable; no one saw it coming. The situation that's in front of us is far from being called an exaggerated consequence of ignoring healthful living. It's quite baffling in this modern age of technology and science, that the one assurance we have of escaping this hell of a virus is the simple practice of 'hand washing' and maintaining basic hygiene.

Man are social creatures, beings that cannot survive alone. We were taught and have also experienced firsthand that we need another of our kind around us. But we never learned how to deal with a situation like now. We were never trained on how we should cope or what our mental or emotional state should be in at a time when maintenance of 6 feet distance becomes the new norm. The unexpected turn of events have flipped our lives upside down.

Sadly, Covid-19 has robbed us of many things; some of which can never be retrieved. But life must go on. We are creatures of adaptability. We have to somehow keep up and still survive. We must continue to provide and receive education. The teaching earning process is important more than ever. We need to keep learning; be it through online classes or other informal sources. We cannot afford to be that 'lost' generation whose future was snatched unapologetically by Lady Corona. It won't be the loss of this generation alone but the effects will be seen in the years to come; like how in the present we are facing the after-effects of the ignorance caused by the lack of education of the generations before us. Thus, in times like now education is what will make the difference. This is not the hour for us to laze around and become stagnant deliberating that we have much time on our hands to spare given the scenario of the enforced lockdown; that we can do as we desire or rest to our content. But the wise thing to do instead would be to take it as a challenge and turn it into an opportunity to keep learning and exploring the vast realm of our own mind, thoughts and ideas; more than ever the perfect time to delve deeper into our own self and come out of this pandemic as an evolved, better than ever or so to say an updated or upgraded version of ourselves. There will be light at the end of this tunnel.

In a time when rationality and positivity become a luxury, we are kept sane by an understanding of the system or the way how things work, which is a result of our education. One thing that is clearly visible amongst this dark cloud of gloom is the impact that education has in trying to subdue the problem. We can clearly see how education has a significant hand in the search for the solution. There is difference in how an educated and literate individual or society handles this pandemic and how the vice versa does it.

Also, the ability or willingness to trust and follow the system, the various guidelines laid down by various experts also fall under the wide range of education; the way someone deals with this crisis gives a broad, overall picture of the mindset of that individual stemming from the quality of education received.

Hence education can and should never be betrayed. Education will in fact save human kind. But the fear that's dawned upon us has put us in an overwhelming state of panic and helplessness. In this war between nature and humanity; what often feels like a lost battle, we still need to remember to breathe and develop a firm mindset that we are going to walk out, even crawl if need be out of the darkness within, hanging onto the thin shred of hope and determination that we will persevere.

As a student of DM College of Teacher Education and as future educator it becomes a duty of mine to help those around be aware of what and how we can deal in such a crisis. Neither the order of the government nor their policies will be as effective unless we as responsible individuals do our part as well and prevent the spread. It will be the collective effort of the people and their strive that will overcome this pandemic.

It is high time that we also educate ourselves and those around us about mental health and its importance. Many are suffering from anxiety and depression due to this sudden change in our lifestyles and we need to learn how to cope and adapt. With fear and sickness and death around us, it becomes impossible for us to have a bright outlook on life and the world around us. We must try to become a beacon of light for ourselves, if not for others, so that we may not lose ourselves; so that our mental status and emotional health is not shattered. Our 'firm' mindset may waver at times because we are ,after all, sensitive beings. But the important thing is knowing how to get back on track even if it takes a while.

As educated individuals it is our responsibility to see ourselves as resources and contribute whatever possible to the welfare of our society. With hope for humanity and faith in medical science, I pray and wish for this dreaded disease to come to an end soon.

Life has to go on.

---------*-------

Intentionally Left Blank

---------*-------

RELEGATION

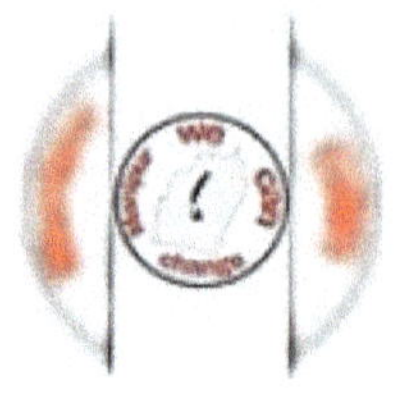

BY NGRISTIN LUKRAM

WE CAN CHANGE MANIPUR-WCCM

wccm2024 'RELEGATION'

I have a photograph
Of us in our prime
Treasured reminder
Of happier times.
Why did you leave me
Three months ago?
I gave you everything
You wanted and more
Shared your dreams
Made some come true
Created new illusions
All for you
Where are you now?
Do you think of me?
Or, am I relegated to,
Insignificant memory?

–Ngristin Lukram

#wecanchangemanipur

19 June 2021

---------*-------

Intentionally Left Blank

---------*-------

SEE THE POSITIVE IN NEGATIVE

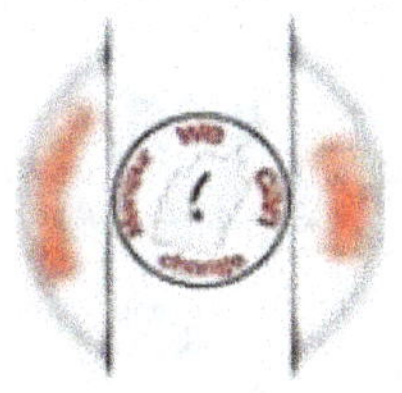

BY LUMREICHAN NK

WE CAN CHANGE MANIPUR-WCCM

wccm2024 'See The Positive In Negative'

It's good to get our heart broken
sometimes so that we understand
and feel the broken ones.
It's good to be deprived of luxuries
so that we understand and feel the poor.
It's good to be judged sometimes so that
we understand how people feel when we judge
them.
It's good to be left alone sometimes so
that we acknowledge and appreciate the people
around us.

– Lumreichan NK

#wecanchangemanipur
View all 2 comments
19 June 2021

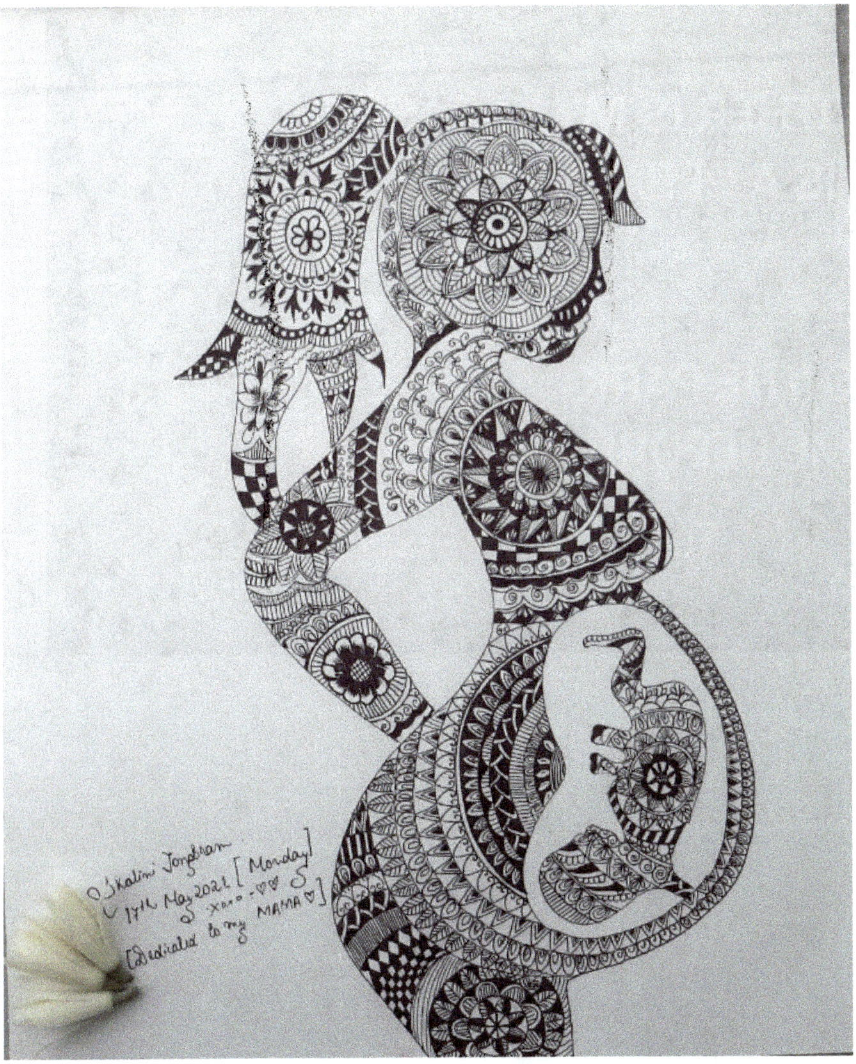

© Shalini Jongbram
17th May 2021 [Monday]
xoxo
[Dedicated to my MAMA♡]

wccm2024 MY MOTHER IS MY TREASURE
BEING WITH HER IS A PLEASURE
SHE GOES CRAZY
WHEN I'M LAZY
SHE TAKES ME TO THE PARK
AND RETURN HOME BEFORE IT'S DARK❤️

– Shalini Tongbram

---------*-------

Intentionally Left Blank

---------*-------

TARAMDAI NUMIT

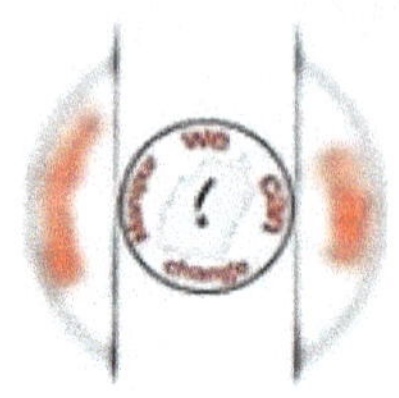

BY ROTIKA HAOBAM

WE CAN CHANGE MANIPUR-WCCM

wccm2024 'TARAMDAI NUMIT'

Phamli ka adugi kachin amada
Mamsanlakee
Ouba phangdey eshana eshabu
Yengjabata natana
Lapna Ouriba
Ngangleinaba machuna phijang oi,
Hayeng kouba magidamak potharurage
Haina changkhi masaigonda
Engna lemna kayada phajariba
'Taramdaigi numit'.
Thamoida chakliba meichak asisu
Mathanta mutchakhigadra natraga Eigisu
'HAYENG' haiba asha ama thamlaga
Awabase thabunungda thamjankhrasira..
Taramdaigi numitsu
Eigi thamoigi meichaksu
Animak erol nungda lupkhigadava
Ngaktani...
Khetnaribadi
Eig thamoigi meichakti
Taibangpanba amatana khngdey.

– Rotika Haobam
(RJ7).

---------*-------

Intentionally Left Blank

---------*-------

TENGOT MACHA

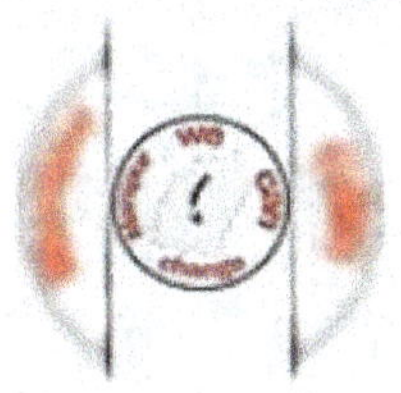

BY KORIMAYUM JONEYZIAUR RAHMAN

WE CAN CHANGE MANIPUR-WCCM

wccm2024 'Tengot Macha'

Harao Harao Barton do yabirakhi
Masak khangdaba mamannaba ahum ga loinarakhi
alto car duda
Eikhoigi math takpa eina toina haiba Sir Jackson
du ni haina
emada sak takchakhi
Car tongba mee lak aena manap choba
phuwaonaba eikhoigi
angang mayamdo thongjin mapanda Eid ki peisa
ninaba
koisang snglei
Yam Haokhre Yam Haokhre na oja ga magi
marupsinggana
haibadu tabada eisu adukki matik Haraojakhi
Eid Nonganbaga numit nini Puksi Hajam oidena
eidi school su
karudre

Mathangi numitta Ahumsuba class ta Sir Jackson na Duster
amaga Math ki Guide lairik ama pairaga class ta chngakee
Emana thongba Sansa gi mahaodo soidana mayam mamangda
thagatlakkani haibasi eingonda phaokhi
Ojaduna eingonda yenglakaaga Rahman nakhoigi tengot to
piktakna madu da yaoba Saa matum ahum do onthokna
haokhre hairakpa
Class ta phamlamba emannaba emannabi mayamduna Waaa
haina nokee

Ojaduna amuk makha tarakee eidi chandi chapi shu
yaohoudadana tara tara yenbada lupa 100 loikhiba khnghoude
Amuk Class ta phamlamba emannaba emannabi mayamduna
Waaa haina nokee
Ekaibana mai thangatpa ngamkhide mana
Pythagoras theorem
takpado ei kokta changkhide
Oja thokkhraga khara phagadra khanbani ekaibase Oja
thokkhraba matungdadi emannabasingna thengot macha
tengot macha na laosallakpado
Nakongda chahi chuppa jang jang laona nillaga leikhi
Kari nungi matamsigi chatnabi khangdraba lairaba pidat padatpa
eina oja ado barton toujaruribano na ningamdaba phaokhi

– Korimayum Joneyziaur Rahman

#wecanchangemanipur

View all 4 comments

29 May 2021 · **See translation**

---------*-------

Intentionally Left Blank

---------*-------

THE MEMORIES OF MY CHILDHOOD FRIEND

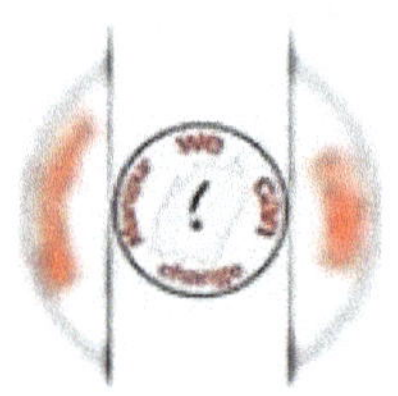

BY JANENDRA LEISHANGTHEM

WE CAN CHANGE MANIPUR-WCCM

wccm2024 “The Memories Of My
Childhood Friend”

Time goes continuously just like a flowing River
stop.
A flowing Rivers may stop when the rain stop.
But time never delay, it goes like stop wind blows.
And the passed memories of my childhood are still
in my
heart.
Sometimes I played and took recreation of my
mind with
them.
Sometimes I laughed with them by remembering
those
days we cried.
Sometimes I cried with them by remembering
those days
we laughed.

Those special memories of my life will always
bring a
smile.
If only I could have you back for just a little
moment.
Then we could laugh and smile just like we used to
do in
childhood.
And the fact that you are no more causes me pain
in heart.
My childhood memories are timeless treasure in
my heart.
But the memories of childhood are still forever in
my heart.
Until I reach the moment of death.

– Janendra Leishangthem

#wecanchangemanipur

12 June 2021

---------*-------

Intentionally Left Blank

---------*-------

THE HARBOUR

BY FELICIFER

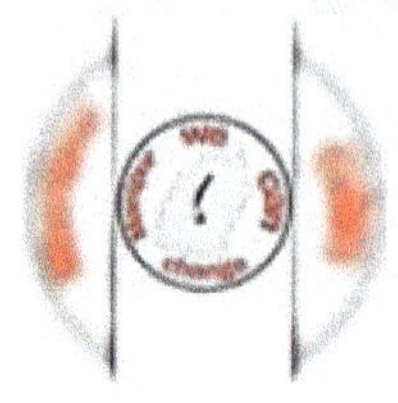

WE CAN CHANGE MANIPUR-WCCM

wccm2024 'The Harbour'

The harbour seems tense
For the breeze carries a sense,
Of the forthcoming calamity
Brought by those enmity.
Once this harbour was calm
And there was no need for alm.
Like the jewel worn by the royal
The harbour stands tall and loyal.
Now the people here has change
The harbour becoming strange.
From the words of their rivalries
Without bothering their policies,
Brothers draw swords upon each other
Forgetting they have the same mother.
Alas! The calm here is gone
To be replace by this eerie tone.
The harbour seems tense
For the breeze carries a sense,
Of the forthcoming calamity
Brought by those enmity.

– Felicefer

#wecanchangemanipur

29 May 2021

---------*-------

Intentionally Left Blank

---------*-------

THE WHITE MOSAIC

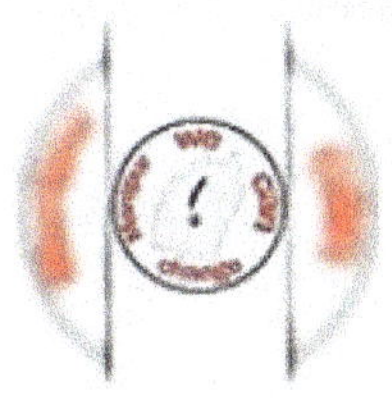

BY LUMREICHAN N.K.

WE CAN CHANGE MANIPUR-WCCM

"THE WHITE MOSAIC"

By Lumreichan NK

The White Mosaic always envied the others. They seemed more special, colorful, dazzling. While, he was just plain white.

"Will any buyers ever show their interest in me?" He asked his artist wistfully.

"Don't worry, my dear. You are special and you will find that out very soon." She assured.

Then, came the sales day. Customers flooded in and they all rushed to sing praises for the multicolored mosaics.

"WOW! She is such a Renaissance Mosaic!," exclaimed a customer.

"I love him! He will add aesthetics to my living room," said another.

No one glanced at the White Mosaic.

Minutes turned into hours and the sales had to be closed. Nonetheless, the customers were so engaged with the mosaics that they didn't hear the artist tell them that they had to make a choice.

"Attention please! It appears that you didn't hear me earlier. I shall repeat. Kindly make your choices. It is time to end the sales." She repeated.

Frantically, they went from one mosaic to another, unable to decide which to buy. Some called up their friends, spouses describing each mosaic and which to buy. Some appeared to have made their decision while some were still in confusion. Then, on the spur of the moment, many of them came rushing to the White Mosaic.

"I'll take him. I realized I don't really need the others but I need this one for my floors and walls." Said one.

"Oh come on! Don't you want colorful floors and walls? This is too plain. I am just thinking of buying it because no other color goes along with my purple kitchen walls. Otherwise, I wouldn't buy it too." Said another foxily.

"I need it for my bathroom too. The colorful ones hide the dirt so I need this plain white one. Please let me buy it." Begged another. A couple others chimed in and the bargaining went on to no avail.

The artist had no choice but to interrupt.

"I see your equal interest for my White Mosaic but currently, I only have one of his kind. Therefore, you will have to place your order and come back some other day." Declared the artist firmly.

Those who wanted to buy the colorful mosaics, bought them and left happily. While, the ones interested in the White Mosaic placed their orders and left dejectedly.

When all left, the White Mosaic, asked his artist hopefully- "Does it mean I am also special?"

"Yes, of course darling. You are special. Don't you realize that you are a need and not a want? That's very special." Responded the artist in a bittersweet manner. She wished he knew his importance. She wished he had more confidence.

"But I am just plain white." Said the White Mosaic, still skeptical.

"White or colorful, I have created all of you differently with a different purpose in mind. You are adjustable in a way that you go well with any color. While, the others may not be that adjustable but bring glamour wherever they're placed. You are all beautiful and special in your own ways. So, don't ever compare with each other."

The White Mosaic slept peacefully that night knowing he is also special and has a purpose. He also dreamt of his brothers and sisters. They were all laughing and playing together without being envious of one another.

---------*-------

Intentionally Left Blank

---------*-------

WAKE UP KANGLEICHA

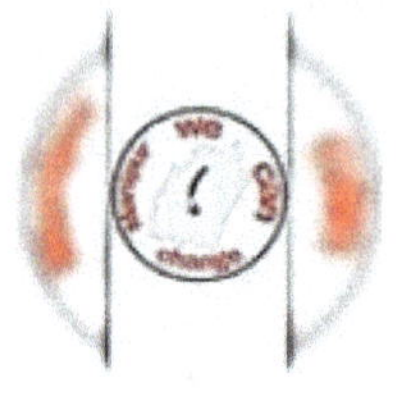

BY BORUN NANDEIBAM

WE CAN CHANGE MANIPUR-WCCM

wccm2024 "Wake Up Kangleicha"

Freedom as if we are held captive to our future
Days, years passed, time
To shed off false convictions
So that the truth can unfold
We are small hamlet, for there is our past jotted down
Still swotting other's beliefs
As if we are a mysteries
Beings, Own customs needs to be Light up
Lets wake up Kangleicha
For we are the outnumbered
The one and only Meitei
Needs to be saved for there
Is still Time

– Borun Nandeibam

5 June 2021

---------*-------

Intentionally Left Blank

---------*-------

WHY WE GIRLS

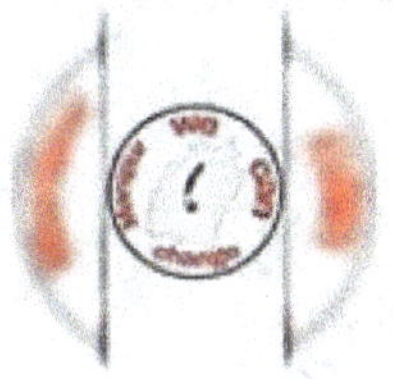

BY AMISHA SOIBAM

WE CAN CHANGE MANIPUR-WCCM

wccm2024 "WHY WE GIRLS ???"

WHY only us ? OR
WHY only I ?
WHY we have to be targeted ?
WHY we need to always compromise ?
WHY we need to always sacrifice ?
WHY we need to think about others before stepping ?
WHY we can"t do anything of our own ?
WHY we can"t get a chance to choose ?
WHY we can"t decide ?
WHY we need to think about our society ?
WHY this so called "SOCIETY" is made ?
WHO made this SOCIETY ?
WHO run this SOCIETY?
WHY SOCIETY rules over us ?
Being born as a girl was a curse or a mistake
I"m not heartless OR we"re not heartless
WE girls have heart , I too have heart
PLEASE give us a chance to do what we want
Listen to us once only once.............
(DO boys also go through all these or we girls only ?)
– Amisha Soibam

View all 5 comments

5 June 2021

---------*-------

Intentionally Left Blank

---------*-------

WOMEN EMPOWERMENT AND IT'S DRAWBACK

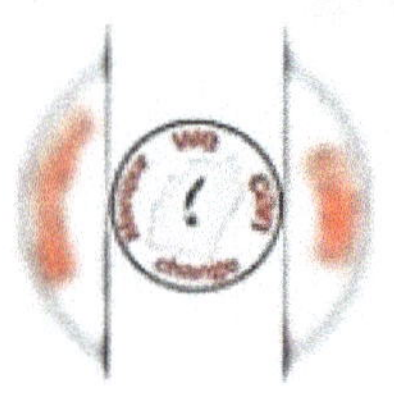

BY KONSAM KELVIN

WE CAN CHANGE MANIPUR-WCCM

'Women empowerment and its drawback'

By Konsam Kevin

The men and women are both equal, unique and difference in experience and both are important for bringing influence in decision making process.

The leadership of women in public sector shows the development of nation. The equal right of men and women in the society improve the work quality and thus the economic status of the nation.

India is a democratic country and historically, India is male dominated country. The men are means half power of the country and they are walking alone, forcing women to do household works. They don't know that women are half power of the country and if male and female combine can form full power of the country. The Indian men never realised the power of the Indian women, in fact women are more powerful than men.

There is a need to change the mentally of everyone that women are weak and they can't do anything.

The issues like women backwards in India such as gender based violence, reproductive health inequalities, economic discrimination, harmful traditional practices and other pervasive and persistent form of inequality.

Moreover, women have a lot of pressure from the parents, society and they are forced to be the main caregiver, caretaker of all the family members. In India it is very challenging to bring changes about women in traditional society. It can be changed but it will take time and regular efforts. A large effort has been made to include women in school to better their education. Similarly, it also focuses on empowering women and girls to achieve gender equality through equal access to various type of opportunities. Women empowerment can be measured through gender empowerment measure, which show women participation in given nation both politically and economically, other measures include: gender parity index or the gender related development index. Women have served in various senior official position in Indian government, that of the president of India, prime minister of India, speaker of Lok Sabha. The rate of malnutrition is exceptionally high among adolescent girls, pregnant and lactating women in India with the repercussion for children's health. Violence against women, especially sexual violence, has been on the rise in India.

Beti Bachao Beti Padhao is a campaign of the government that aims to generate awareness and improve the efficiency of the welfare services intended for girls in India. According to the census data in India, the child sex ratio was 927 girls per 1000 boys in 2001 which dropped to 918 girls for every 1000 boys in 2011.

The situation seems to be a little bit of contrasting in context of northeast, women are much empowerment leading the protest from the front. We have local market specially designated for the women like ema market or the local meira paibis (organisation working to safeguard the society) playing a crucial role in the community works. Or sometimes I may not be wrong to say that men empowerment has also become an important topic to discuss on especially in such area.

On such crucial matter, there shouldn't be any politics. Still women in the society are being tortured mentally and physically harassed or being treated illiterally. Country can only be developed when both men and women are treated equally without any prejudice.

But in the last few years, cases of women misusing their rights has come into effect causing a big blow to the cause of women empowerment.

Women tends to forget the basic principle behind this great cause of empowering women.

By saying so much in favour of women, I'm also in agreement that discrimination exist against men and boys as well. Men are also victims of domestic violence and sexual assault and social discrimination but state institution and society take such violence less seriously because of prevailing attitude against men .

No law should be misused by anyone. An allegation by women is not enough to defame the reputation of men in the society.

Rightly said, crime has no gender and the statement "to be born a man in India is a crime. And to marry an Indian girl is a heinous crime. And this is because of anti-men laws in the name of laws to protect women" is rightly justifiable.

---------*-------

Intentionally Left Blank

---------*-------

A PSYCHIATRIST? BUT WHY, I'M PERFECTLY FINE

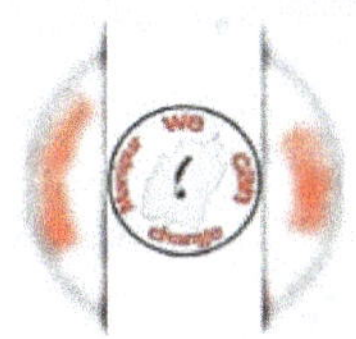

BY YAIPHABI MAYENGBAM

WE CAN CHANGE MANIPUR-WCCM

"A Psychiatrist? But Why, I'm Perfectly Fine"

by Yaiphabi Mayengbam

As the title portrays, this article centres around the main theme of 'mental health', focusing on the context of students. Applying a bit of common sensical knowledge allows us to identify psychological factors as the cause of mental health problems. However, a view from a sociological perspective points out, in addition, social factors for the cause of the same. These can be listed as gender, social class, race, disability, etc., and the social inequalities associated with them. Diverting from the general analysis, here, the focus is on students and their mental health. 'Competition' stealing the spotlight of their life stage, places a huge burden on their shoulders of having to meet the expectations from the social beings around them. Having said this, it is easy to imply that students, especially those candidates appearing in board and public competitive exams, are, in most cases, troubled with tension, anxiety and depression under the umbrella term 'mental illness'.

Here, it is well aware on the part of both the students and parents/guardians that the best and effective way to restore one's mental health is to receive psychological treatment and counseling from a psychiatrist or an expert in the field.

However, the social stigma revolving around people's mindset regarding such treatment plays a big role in hindering students from accepting the fact that they need to consult a psychiatrist. They tend to reassert the fact that they are not in any way suffering from mental health problems and keep denying treatment, when this denial, in fact, aggravates their condition.

So, one important point, students and others concerned should stress on, is that mental health should be looked at from a similar viewpoint as in the case of physical health. Whenever our physical health is affected in any way, the foremost step we undertake is to consult a physician and undergo treatment accordingly. Here, damage to our physical health is not at all perceived as a disability. Likewise, disruptions affecting mental health leading to mental health problems should not be considered as some kind of severe disability and it is really important and necessary to normalize receiving treatment from a psychiatrist or counsellor. However, an issue on the dark side of this process is the high treatment charges which becomes a barrier to people who cannot afford them. This is also another social factor which keeps people back from receiving such treatment. Hence, 'mental health' should be prioritized if we are to aim for a good foundation of the future society. More awareness on this social issue can be raised among the general public and this particular article desires to serve that purpose.

---------*-------

Intentionally Left Blank

---------*-------

WCCM is thankful to:

Go Green Group, Manipur

Lamjing Meira

Laihui Ensemble, Imphal

Kihom, Manipur

Mitsna, Manipur

Thawai Hou Arts & Event, Pvt. Ltd., Manipur

StoryTeller, Imphal

Meira Foods, Manipur

Mayanglambam family (Maibam Rebika Devi, Mayanglambam Mangangsana)

Students of Laihui's Pp (Play Pena) Class, Imphal

Parents of Laihui's Pp Class, Imphal

Ex-Members of WCCM

Members of WCCM

Families and relatives of WCCM's Members

Well-wishers of WCCM

------------#wccm2024--------

Instagram: @wccm2024

Email: wecanchangemanipur@gmail.com

Looking forward to a Peaceful Manipur soon.

www.ingramcontent.com/pod-product-compliance
Lightning Source LLC
Chambersburg PA
CBHW080025260726
48658CB00007B/2482
9798871913062